ANTARCTICA
EXPLORATION

GREG REID

To Kathy, Steve, Sam and Mia.

This edition first published in 2005 in the United States of America by Smart Apple Media.
All rights reserved. No part of this book may be reproduced in any form or by any means without written permission from the Publisher.

Smart Apple Media
1980 Lookout Drive
North Mankato
Minnesota 56003

First published in 2005 by
MACMILLAN EDUCATION AUSTRALIA PTY LTD
627 Chapel Street, South Yarra, Australia 3141

Visit our website at www.macmillan.com.au

Associated companies and representatives throughout the world.

Copyright © Greg Reid 2005

Library of Congress Cataloging-in-Publication Data
Reid, Greg, 1955-
    Exploration / by Greg Reid.
    p. cm. – (Antarctica)
    ISBN 1-58340-762-6
    1. Antarctica—Discovery and exploration—Juvenile literature. I. Title.
    G863.R39 2005
    919.8′9—dc22

2005042586

Edited by Vanessa Lanaway
Text and cover design by Ivan Finnegan, iF Design
Maps by Laurie Whiddon, Map Illustrations
Photo research by Jes Senbergs

Printed in China

Acknowledgments

The author would like to thank the following people for their invaluable help: Angela Berry, Beryl Hansen, Louise Harris, Carmen Galvin, Janine Hanna, Sandra McMullan, Eileen Shuttleworth, Joanna Taylor, Cathryn Williams, Eunice Wong.

The author and the publisher are grateful to the following for permission to reproduce copyright material:

Front cover photographs: Satellite image of the continent of Antarctica, showing areas of thick ice and land but not the permanent ice shelves surrounding the continent, courtesy of Worldsat International/Science Photo Library.

Ski-Doo (left), courtesy of Patricia Selkirk. Mawson's Hut (middle), courtesy of Colin Monteath/Auscape. Apple hut (right), courtesy of AAD.

Back cover photograph: Icebreaker, courtesy of Reg Morgan.

AAD, pp. 20, 28; Colin Monteath/Auscape, pp. 15; 21; Rick Price–Survival Anglia/Auscape, p. 9; Corbis, p. 19; Global Publishing, pp. 16, 17; Len Stewart/Lochman Transparencies, p. 6; Macquarie Net, p. 18; Mary Evans Picture Library, p. 12; Reg Morgan, pp. 22, 30; By permission of the National Library of Australia, pp. 4, 5, 7, 14; Patricia Selkirk, p. 23; Canadian Space Agency/Radarsat/NASA/Science Photo Library, p. 24; NASA/Science Photo Library, pp. 25, 26; Sinclair Stammers/Science Photo Library, p. 27; Joanna Taylor, pp. 8, 29.

Background and header images courtesy of www.istockphoto.com. Frozen Fact background image courtesy of NOAA.

While every care has been taken to trace and acknowledge copyright, the publisher tenders their apologies for any accidental infringement where copyright has proved untraceable. Where the attempt has been unsuccessful, the publisher welcomes information that would redress the situation.

Please note
At the time of printing, the Internet addresses appearing in this book were correct. Owing to the dynamic nature of the Internet, however, we cannot guarantee that all these addresses will remain correct.

Contents

The Antarctic 4
Captain James Cook's voyage 5
Early sealers and whalers 6
Early scientific expeditions 8
Early explorers 10
Race to the South Pole 12
Great Antarctic explorers 14
Exploration by air 16
International exploration agreement 18
Scientific exploration 20
Recent scientific discoveries 24
Antarctic issues 28
The future of the Antarctic 30
Glossary 31
Index 32

GLOSSARY WORDS
When a word is printed in bold, you can look up its meaning in the Glossary on page 31.

Look for this symbol to find links to more information online.

The Antarctic

The Antarctic consists of the frozen continent of Antarctica, the stormy Southern Ocean, and the isolated **sub-Antarctic islands**. The region is the world's last great wilderness and contains unique landscapes, plants, and animals.

Antarctica is one of the harshest environments for life on Earth. It is an island continent that is mostly buried under snow and ice. Antarctica has a thick **ice sheet** and thousands of **valley glaciers**, floating **ice shelves**, ice cliffs, sea ice, and icebergs. Its isolation and cold climate protected it from discovery for many years.

Antarctica was the last of the seven continents to be discovered and explored. The Southern Ocean and the barrier of **pack ice** surrounding Antarctica kept it hidden until 1820. Scientific exploration since the 1830s has unlocked many secrets of the Antarctic, and research continues today. The continent has become a unique place of international cooperation. Managing the Antarctic is a major issue for all countries, both now and in the future.

For centuries, maps referred to Antarctica as *Terra Australis Nondum Cognita* (Unknown Southern Land).

FROZEN FACT

ANCIENT PREDICTION
The ancient Greeks called the constellation of stars above the northern sky *Arctos* or "the bear," so they called the southern continent *Antarktikos* or "opposite the bear."

Captain James Cook's voyage

In 1772, British explorer Captain James Cook was sent to search for Antarctica. Cook's voyage was the first to cross the Antarctic Circle, but the explorers never saw Antarctica.

Cook's voyage lasted three years. His crew sailed in small ships called the *Resolution* and the *Adventure*. The ships had double wooden hulls to protect them from the ice. Cook crossed the Antarctic Circle four times. He was the first to **circumnavigate** Antarctica and prove that it lay south of the Antarctic Circle. Cook also discovered several sub-Antarctic islands, such as South Georgia and the South Sandwich Islands.

http://www.enchantedlearning.com/explorers/antarctica.shtml

http://library.thinkquest.org/26442/html/explore/index.html

When he returned to England, Cook told stories of giant icebergs, pack ice, thick fogs, dangerous seas, and plentiful wildlife. Cook was sure that the source of most of the ice in the Southern Ocean was the land around the South Pole. Although his voyage proved that Antarctica was not a green and fertile place, Cook's maps and reports of wildlife encouraged fleets of sealers and whalers to explore the Antarctic.

A painting of Cook's voyage into the Antarctic with the *Resolution* and the *Adventure*.

FROZEN FACT

COOK'S PREDICTION
Cook said that no one would explore further south than him. He also said that this **remote** country was useless, frozen wasteland.

Early sealers and whalers

Seal and whale hunters from Britain and the United States were among the first to discover and explore Antarctica. Until the 1850s, sealers and whalers did much of the exploration in the Antarctic.

EARLY SEALERS

In 1764, the sealing industry started on the Falkland Islands, off the east coast of South America. Sealers discovered and explored many areas of Antarctica and the sub-Antarctic islands while searching for new sealing grounds. In 1819, a British sealer, William Smith, discovered the South Shetland Islands, just north of the Antarctic Peninsula.

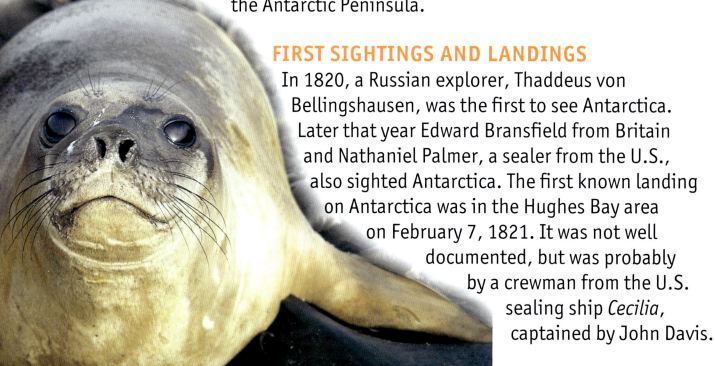

Southern elephant seals were hunted almost to extinction by early sealers.

FIRST SIGHTINGS AND LANDINGS

In 1820, a Russian explorer, Thaddeus von Bellingshausen, was the first to see Antarctica. Later that year Edward Bransfield from Britain and Nathaniel Palmer, a sealer from the U.S., also sighted Antarctica. The first known landing on Antarctica was in the Hughes Bay area on February 7, 1821. It was not well documented, but was probably by a crewman from the U.S. sealing ship *Cecilia*, captained by John Davis.

FROZEN FACT
COST OF EXPLORATION
Sealers pushed some seal **species** to the edge of **extinction** for profit. Seals were hunted for their skins and blubber, which was boiled for its oil.

Early whaling in the Antarctic was extremely dangerous.

JAMES WEDDELL

In 1823, a warmer than usual summer reduced the pack ice around Antarctica. This helped James Weddell, a British sealing ship captain, to sail even farther south than Captain Cook had done 49 years earlier. Weddell discovered the Weddell Sea. It was not until 1841 that another ship would sail this far south.

http://library.thinkquest.org/26442/html/explore/whalers_sealers.html

THE ENDERBY BROTHERS

The Enderby Brothers of London were sealing and whaling businessmen. They encouraged the captains of their ships to explore Antarctica while they hunted seals and whales. In 1831, Enderby Land in East Antarctica was named after them.

SECRETS AND LIES

Many discoveries were kept secret so other sealers would not discover new seal colonies. Some sealers deliberately named and charted islands that did not exist, to trick their competitors.

EARLY WHALERS

Early whalers also explored and mapped parts of the Antarctic while hunting southern right whales for their blubber (fat). In 1839, a British whaler and sealer, John Belleny, discovered the islands that now bear his name. In 1840, he named the Sabrina Coast on Antarctica.

FROZEN FACT
PHANTOM ISLANDS
Early maps showed many non-existent islands in the Southern Ocean. These phantom islands were sometimes deliberately wrong, but others were possibly huge icebergs that looked like islands.

Early scientific expeditions

Between 1838 and 1843, three national scientific expeditions arrived to explore Antarctica. They each wanted to be the first to explore Antarctica, make discoveries, and claim territory for their country.

CAPTAIN DUMONT D'URVILLE

The first expedition was led by a French captain, Dumont d'Urville. It failed to beat James Weddell's record for the most southerly exploration of Antarctica. In 1838, d'Urville mapped parts of the Antarctic Peninsula and the South Shetland Islands. His two ships were trapped in pack ice for five days and the crew had to cut them out. In 1840, d'Urville returned and named Adélie Land after his wife and claimed it for France.

http://www.south-pole.com/p0000077.htm

http://www.south-pole.com/p0000079.htm

LIEUTENANT CHARLES WILKES

Charles Wilkes led the United States Exploring Expedition to Antarctica. It failed to sail further south than Cook and Weddell, and only two of the six ships survived the expedition. Although Wilkes never reached Antarctica, he sighted land. In 1840, Wilkes surveyed more than 1,700 miles (2,700 km) of the pack ice in what is now called Wilkes Land. He was the first explorer to say that Antarctica was a continent.

FROZEN FACT

ADÉLIE PENGUINS
Several Adélie penguins were collected on Dumont d'Urville's 1840 expedition and taken back to France. The species are named after Dumont d'Urville's wife.

CAPTAIN JAMES CLARK ROSS

James Clark Ross led a British expedition from 1839 to 1843. After his success in locating the North Magnetic Pole in 1831, British scientists hoped he would be the first to find the South Magnetic Pole.

Ross had experience in the Arctic and his crew and two sailing ships were well prepared. Although they did not find the South Magnetic Pole, Ross's expedition discovered many new places, made magnetic surveys, collected rocks and plants, and took the first Antarctic sea **soundings**. Ross was the first explorer to break through the pack ice barrier surrounding Antarctica.

http://www.south-pole.com/p0000081.htm

Ross sailed into what is now called the Ross Sea. He named an active volcano on Ross Island, Mount Erebus, and another mountain, Mount Terror, after his ships. Ross found the Ross Ice Shelf, which he charted eastwards for 390 nautical miles (720 km). He found that the edge of the ice shelf floated on the sea. Ross made the first fully documented landing on Antarctica at Possession Island. He named the nearby land Victoria Land and claimed it for Queen Victoria, the reigning Queen of Britain at the time.

Ross marked the Ross Ice Shelf on his chart as the Victoria Barrier after Queen Victoria.

FROZEN FACT

NEAR DISASTER
In 1842, Ross's expedition almost met disaster. His two ships collided and entangled in a storm while trying to avoid an iceberg.

Early explorers

After Ross's expedition, sealers and whalers explored Antarctica for the next 30 years. In 1874, the first steam-powered ship was used to break through the ice barrier around Antarctica. Explorers came from many different nations. They risked their lives and greatly expanded scientific knowledge in many areas.

1 1874
The British ship *Challenger* was the first steam vessel in the Antarctic. The expedition found about 350 new animal species. It also discovered rocks that icebergs had carried from Antarctica and dropped on the sea bed, proving that the ice on Antarctica once covered a greater area.

2 1893
Norwegian, Carl Larsen found the first fossil discovered on Antarctica, at Cape Seymour. Larsen later established Norwegian whaling stations on South Georgia.

3 1895
A Norwegian expedition organised by Henryk Bull landed in Cape Adare on Antarctica. This opened the way for land explorations of Antarctica. They found lichens—the first plant life found on Antarctica.

4 1898

Adrien de Gerlache of Belgium and the crew of the *Belgica* were the first to survive an Antarctic winter trapped in ice. They were the first to take winter temperature measurements of Antarctica.

5 1899–1900

Carsten Borchgrevink, a Norwegian-born Australian, led the British Antarctic Expedition aboard the *Southern Cross*. This expedition was the first to spend a winter on Antarctica in timber huts.

6 1901–03

Erich von Drygalski led a German expedition from 1901–03. He named Wilhelm II Land in East Antarctica. Their ship, the *Gauss* was stuck in the ice for 11 months.

7 1901–04

Robert Falcon Scott led the British National Antarctic Expedition from 1901–04. He was the first person to fly over Antarctica in a hydrogen balloon.

8 1901–04

Otto Nordenskjöld led the Swedish South Polar Expedition from 1901–04. Six scientists spent two years on Snow Hill Island. Their ship, the *Antarctic* sank and the crew survived by eating penguins and their eggs. An Argentinean ship rescued them.

9 1902–04

William Bruce led the Scottish National Expedition from 1902–04. He set up a base on the South Orkney Islands. Bruce also explored and named Coats Land. The expedition researched marine life of the Weddell Sea and wildlife on the South Orkney Islands.

10 1903–05 1908–10

Jean-Baptiste Charcot led two French Antarctic Expeditions in 1903–05 and 1908–10. He charted 1,240 miles (2,000 km) of the western Antarctic Peninsula and named Charcot Land after his father.

11 1909

Sir Douglas Mawson and Edgeworth David of Australia, and Alistair Mackay of Britain were part of the British Antarctic Expedition of 1907–09. They were the first to reach the area of the South Magnetic Pole. They traveled by **sled** from Ross Island to Victoria Land.

12 1910–12

Nobu Shirase led the Japanese South Polar Expedition from 1910–12. Using dog sleds they traveled nearly 186 miles (300 km) on the Antarctic Plateau. They had wanted to reach the South Pole, but Roald Amundsen and Robert Scott beat them.

13 1911–12

Wilhelm Filchner led the Second German Antarctic Expedition from 1911–12. They set up a base on an ice shelf and had to rescue the material and animals when it broke off and drifted away.

Race to the South Pole

The next challenge was to reach the South Pole. In 1909, Ernest Shackleton's British team came within 99 miles (160 km) of the pole. In 1911, Roald Amundsen of Norway and Robert Falcon Scott of Britain led expeditions to claim the prize.

AMUNDSEN'S VICTORY

Amundsen was an experienced Antarctic explorer who planned his expedition in secret. He sailed to the Bay of Whales and set up a base called Framheim. It was at the other end of the Ross Ice Shelf to Scott's base and 60 miles (97 km) closer to the South Pole.

Amundsen was well organized. Before starting out, his team set up food **depots** along the route. Five men and 52 dogs left on October 19, 1911. They used skis and teams of huskies to pull sleds. They reached the South Pole on December 14, 1911. After 99 days and 683 miles (1,093 km), the men and 12 dogs returned safely to Framheim. Five days later they sailed to Tasmania to tell the world of their victory.

http://home.earthlink.net/%7Ekcrawfish/amundsen.html

Amundsen and his men raised the Norwegian flag at the South Pole and left a letter to the King of Norway, some clothes, and a **sextant** in a tent.

FROZEN FACT

AMUNDSEN'S SECRET DiET
Amundsen's team ate wholemeal bread, berry preserves, and undercooked seal and penguin meat. They did not starve or have any deficiencies in their diet.

SCOTT'S DISASTER

Scott was also an experienced Antarctic explorer. He conducted his second attempt to reach the South Pole in 1911–12. Scott arrived on the *Terra Nova* and set up his base at Cape Evans.

http://library.thinkquest.org/26442/html/explore/comparison.html

Scott's team laid out food depots along the route, but the final food depot (One Ton Depot) was 36 miles (58 km) short of where it should have been. Scott and four other men left Cape Evans on October 24, 1911. They traveled slowly on skis, pulling their sleds. Scott's team reached the South Pole on January 17, 1912 only to find that Amundsen had beaten them by one month.

Unfortunately, all of Scott's team died on the return journey. Edgar Evans died after several bad falls. Lawrence Oates had badly frostbitten feet and walked away from the tent never to be seen again. A blizzard stopped Bowers, Wilson, and Scott 11 miles (18 km) away from One Ton Depot. All three died in their tent. Scott's last diary entry was on March 29, 1912.

Amundsen's and Scott's routes to the South Pole

Key
— Amundsen's expedition 1910–12
— Scott's expedition 1910–13

FROZEN FACT

SCOTT'S MISTAKES
* Dog teams would have traveled faster than men on skis pulling sleds.
* Bowers had no skis and slowed the team down.
* They only had enough food for four people, not five.
* A day was wasted collecting rock specimens on the way back.
* One Ton Depot was put in the wrong place.

Great Antarctic explorers

Shackleton and Mawson were two great Antarctic explorers of the 1900s. Both led expeditions to Antarctica that increased our knowledge of the frozen continent.

LIEUTENANT ERNEST SHACKLETON

Shackleton's first Antarctic expedition was with Robert Scott in 1901. In 1907–09 he attempted to reach the South Pole, but turned back only 99 miles (160 km) away because of a lack of food.

http://home.earthlink.net/%7Ekcrawfish/shackleton.html

http://www.salariya.com/web_books/explorer/index.html

Shackleton's ship, the *Endurance* was crushed in pack ice.

In 1914, Shackleton returned to cross Antarctica by land. The expedition failed, but their amazing survival story shows Shackleton's great leadership.

Shackleton's ship, the *Endurance*, was trapped in pack ice for 10 months before being crushed. The men sailed the ship's three small lifeboats to Elephant Island, but there was no one there. Shackleton and five men took a lifeboat to get help from a whaling station on South Georgia Island. The settlement was over 800 miles (1,290 km) away across dangerous seas. Fortunately, they made it to South Georgia safely. Shackleton returned in a Chilean tugboat and rescued the other men from Elephant Island. All of Shackleton's team survived.

FROZEN FACT

GREAT LEADER
Shackleton was a great expedition leader and a hero in Britain. He died on South Georgia in 1922 on his final expedition to Antarctica and is buried there.

SIR DOUGLAS MAWSON

Mawson was Australia's greatest Antarctic explorer. He was a **geologist** who was part of Shackleton's 1907–09 expedition to the South Magnetic Pole.

Mawson led the Australasian Antarctic Expedition from 1911–14. He set up base camp at Cape Denison on Commonwealth Bay, and explored, named, and mapped the coastal area of Antarctica to the south of Australia. Mawson's team found the first meteorite on Antarctica. His expedition was the first to use radio communication in Antarctica when, in 1912, they exchanged radio messages between Cape Denison and Macquarie Island.

http://www.mawsons-huts.com.au/history.html

Unfortunately, in 1913–14, Mawson's expedition met with disaster. One of Mawson's companions, Belgrave Ninnas, fell down a **crevasse** with the food supply sled, the main tent, and some dogs. A few months later, Mawson's other companion, Dr Xavier Mertz, died of sickness and frostbite. Mawson fell down a crevasse, but managed to pull himself out. Exhausted and starving, Mawson barely survived the 99 mile (160 km) return trip alone to Cape Denison. He spent the long winter recovering.

FROZEN FACT
MAWSON'S HUT
Mawson called the hut at Cape Denison on Commonwealth Bay "The home of the blizzard." The Australian government restored the hut as an important part of the **cultural heritage** of Antarctica.

Exploration by air

Air exploration of Antarctica started with balloon flights. However, the balloons were tied to the ground for safety reasons. Airplanes increased the area of Antarctica that could be explored and mapped from the air.

http://www.south-pole.com/p0000106.htm

In 1902, British explorers Robert Scott and Ernest Shackleton were the first to see Antarctica from the air in a hydrogen balloon called *Eva*. Shackleton took the first aerial photographs in Antarctica from *Eva*. The same year, German explorer Erich von Drygalski was the first to fly a hot air balloon over Antarctica.

Sir George Hubert Wilkins was the first person to fly an airplane in Antarctic skies.

SIR GEORGE HUBERT WILKINS

Wilkins was an Australian pilot and explorer who was part of Shackleton's 1922 expedition. In 1928, Wilkins and his American co-pilot, Carl Eilson, became the first to fly an airplane over part of Antarctica. The 11-hour flight covered more than 1,300 miles (2,100 km) from Deception Island to the Antarctic Peninsula and back.

Wilkins was excited about the value of the airplane in Antarctic exploration. He said, "for the first time in human history, new land was being discovered from the air."

FROZEN FACT

FIRST AIRPLANE IN ANTARCTICA
Douglas Mawson brought the first airplane to Antarctica in 1911. It never flew because the wings were damaged. However, the body and engine were used to tow supplies on the ground.

ADMIRAL RICHARD BYRD

Byrd led several major Antarctic expeditions for the U.S. from 1928–47. In 1929, he and three companions were the first to fly over the South Pole and back on a 19-hour flight. On later expeditions, Byrd's team mapped huge areas of unknown land from the air, and land-based explorers conducted scientific research on the rocks and meteorites of Antarctica. Their Little America II base was on the Ross Ice Shelf.

http://library.thinkquest.org/26442/html/explore/mechanised.html?tqskip1=1

http://www.south-pole.com/p0000107.htm

http://www.south-pole.com/p0000110.htm

Lincoln Ellsworth's plane, the *Polar Star* was the first to complete a trans-Antarctic flight.

LINCOLN ELLSWORTH

Ellsworth was a millionaire adventurer from the U.S. In 1953, in the *Polar Star*, he became the first person to fly across the Antarctic continent. Ellsworth and his co-pilot Herbert Hollick-Kenyon started at Dundee Island, off the northern Antarctic Peninsula. After landing three times, the airplane ran out of fuel and was forced to land on the Ross Ice Shelf. They were about half an hour from their destination at Byrd's Little America II base. Ellsworth, his co-pilot, and their plane were rescued with help from Australia.

Olympics Heights School

FROZEN FACT
SPY IN THE SKY
Modern airplanes that carry radio echo sounding equipment have discovered lakes and mountain ranges buried beneath the Antarctic ice sheet. Satellites also keep watch on changes to the thickness of the ice sheet.

International exploration agreement

The U.S. built the Amundsen-Scott base at the South Pole during the International Geophysical Year.

Until the late-1950s, there was little cooperation between nations exploring Antarctica, and some conflict over territorial claims. However, most nations agreed that future scientific exploration of Antarctica required international cooperation.

INTERNATIONAL GEOPHYSICAL YEAR

From July 1957 until December 1958, a time of international cooperation took place called the International Geophysical Year (IGY). During this time, 12 nations built 50 research bases in Antarctica. Scientists cooperated on many research projects and the success of the IGY led to a move for a permanent agreement on Antarctica.

http://www.antarctica.ac.uk/About_Antarctica/Treaty/

http://en.wikipedia.org/wiki/International_Geophysical_Year

THE ANTARCTIC TREATY

In 1959, the 12 nations that took part in the IGY signed the Antarctic Treaty, agreeing that Antarctica would be free and peaceful. The treaty came into force in 1961, and made Antarctica a unique place in the world.

The Antarctic Treaty does not recognize any territorial claims. Under the treaty, Antarctica became "a continent for peace and science." The treaty bans military activity and supports scientific cooperation. It also outlines rules for exploration to ensure that Antarctica remains a pristine wilderness.

FROZEN FACT

REMOTE BASE

During the IGY, the former Union of Soviet Socialist Republics (now Russia) set up Vostok base at the Pole of Inaccessibility. This is the farthest place from all the coastlines of Antarctica.

THE FIRST LAND CROSSING OF ANTARCTICA

During the International Geophysical Year, Dr. Vivian Fuchs of Britain led the first expedition to cross Antarctica by land. Fuchs and Sir Edmund Hillary, from New Zealand, led two teams starting at opposite ends of the continent and met at the South Pole.

Fuchs's team started from the Weddell Sea and headed towards the pole. Hillary laid out supply depots from Scott base on the Ross Sea along the route to the pole. Hillary's team reached the South Pole before Fuchs, becoming only the third group to do so. Fuchs and Hillary then continued on to Scott base where Fuchs's team became the first people to complete a land crossing of Antarctica.

Both teams used over-snow vehicles and air support for food and fuel supplies. Fuchs had four Snocats, three Weasels, and a Muskeg tractor. Hillary had three Ferguson tractors fitted with rubber tracks, and a caravan to live in. The expedition gathered much scientific data on the thickness of the Antarctic ice sheet along the route.

Sir Edmund Hillary met Dr. Vivian Fuchs at the South Pole in 1958 on the first land crossing of Antarctica.

FROZEN FACT

TRIP STATISTICS
The expedition took **99 days** to travel **2,145 miles (3,460 km)** across Antarctica. Fuchs set out on November 24, 1957 and arrived on March 2, 1958.

Scientific exploration

Most Antarctic exploration today is done for scientific research. Scientists and support staff live on research bases for many months. In summer, about 4,000 people live on Antarctic bases and about 1,500 people live there in winter. Other scientists live on research ships and explore the Southern Ocean around Antarctica.

There are 74 permanent international bases on Antarctica, although only 32 of these are open for the summer. Another 20 bases are found on the sub-Antarctic islands. There are also 35 abandoned bases.

SHELTER

Early buildings on Antarctica were made from timber and were very cold. Permanent buildings today are made of special materials to suit the Antarctic climate. The buildings are heated and comfortable.

Early expeditions used pyramid tents, which are suited to windy conditions. These are still used, but some modern expeditions also use buildings called traverse vehicles, which are towed across the ice. They contain sleeping, cooking, storage, and radio areas. Australian expeditions use fiberglass buildings called "apple" huts. These can be extended to make "melons" and other shapes.

Australian scientists use modern "apple" and "melon" huts when they are doing research in the field.

FROZEN FACT
ANTARCTIC TOWN
The U.S. McMurdo base is the largest base in Antarctica. It is the size of a small town, with nearly 100 main buildings and more than 400 vehicles.

CLOTHING

Early explorers wore heavy, bulky clothing that was difficult to move in. Modern explorers wear lightweight clothing, which lets body moisture escape and allows easy movement. Many layers are used to insulate the body.

Clothing must be windproof on Antarctica because of the fierce winds and blizzards. In the sub-Antarctic area, clothing must also be waterproof.

FOOD

Early explorers carried tinned, salted, and dried foods. They also ate fish, seals, penguins and penguin eggs, and some ate their huskies and horses to survive. Their diet often lacked variety and caused health problems.

Today, most food is brought in from outside. Modern explorers have greater variety and a balanced diet. Eggs and vegetables must be kept warm so they do not freeze. On field expeditions, noodles, rice, chocolate, and canned and freeze-dried food are eaten.

COMMUNICATIONS

In the early days, explorers were unable to communicate with their support base or the outside world. Today, it is much easer to communicate worldwide through radio, cell phones, and e-mail.

Thermal boots, thermal underwear, mittens, and goggles are essential in the Antarctic.

http://www.70south.com/resources/bases

http://www.newzeal.com/theme/Bases.htm

FROZEN FACT
FRESH VEGETABLES
Some bases grow their own vegetables using **hydroponics**. Scientists and staff at these bases appreciate the fresh vegetables.

TRANSPORTATION

Modern changes in transportation technology have also helped make life easier and more comfortable for scientists living at research bases.

OCEAN TRANSPORTATION

Early explorers' ships were wooden sailing vessels that sometimes got stuck or crushed in the pack ice. Steel plates were later fastened to the outside of ships' hulls to protect them from the ice. The invention of steam ships helped explorers to sail farther into the pack ice without relying on the wind. Today, ships are steel-hulled with modern fuel engines. Some ships, called icebreakers, have strengthened steel hulls and powerful engines so they can cut through the pack ice.

AIR TRANSPORTATION

Airplanes have made Antarctica easier for scientists and other people to get to. Some airplanes are fitted with special skis instead of wheels. Helicopters operate from many ships and bases. They take people quickly to remote areas and require very little landing space.

Some icebreakers ride up and over the pack ice and the weight of the ship cracks the ice apart.

FROZEN FACT

FIRST HELICOPTER
The first helicopter to fly in Antarctica was a gyrocopter. It was flown on the Byrd Expedition of 1933–35.

LAND TRANSPORTATION

Some early explorers pulled their sleds themselves, but most explorers used skis, and horse and husky teams. Huskies were the main form of transportation for almost a century, until the mid-1970s, when mechanical transportation took over. The last huskies had to leave Antarctica by 1994 because introduced animals are not allowed under the Antarctic Treaty.

http://www.aad.gov.au/default.asp?casid=2424

http://www.antarctica.ac.uk/Living_and_Working/Transport/

Today, travel on land is easier and faster. Scientific bases have some cars, trucks, tractors, and earth-moving equipment. Special vehicles such as Ski-Doos, which are motorized toboggans with rubber tracks and skis, are used to travel around in the field. Four-wheel-drive motorcycles and all-terrain tracked vehicles called Hagglunds can travel over rocky, uneven ground and pull sleds.

NAVIGATION

Early explorers relied on their compass and the position of the sun and stars to navigate. Today, people use modern communication methods such as radios and satellites. Hand-held Global Positioning Systems (GPS) linked into satellites can chart a location to within a few feet.

Ski-Doos are used to transport people and supplies.

FROZEN FACT

ANTI-FREEZE VEHICLES
All vehicles in Antarctica need special fuel and anti-freeze. They carry a first-aid kit, emergency rations, and a radio for communication in case they have an accident.

Recent scientific discoveries

Modern scientific exploration continues to discover many new things about the Antarctic.

LAKE VOSTOK

http://www.70south.com/resources/environment/vostok

In 1966, Lake Vostok was discovered under Russia's Vostok base in the center of the continent. It is the largest of more than 70 freshwater lakes that lie buried under the Antarctic ice sheet.

Lake Vostok has been cut off from the outside environment for millions of years. It may contain ancient, unique, and undiscovered life forms. Scientists have stopped drilling through the ice sheet just short of the lake. They need to figure out how to prevent the lake from being damaged by outside influences before they explore it.

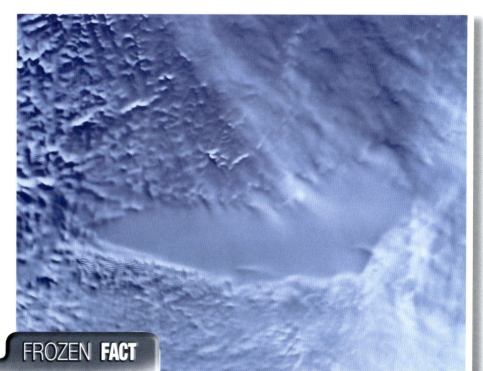

This satellite image shows Lake Vostok, which is buried about 13,200 feet (4,000 m) beneath the ice.

FROZEN FACT

SPACE RESEARCH
The National Aeronautic and Space Administration (NASA) of the U.S. is studying Lake Vostok. They have discovered that the lake is similar to oceans buried under thick layers of ice on Europa, a moon of Jupiter.

PAST ATMOSPHERES

Ice in Antarctica holds some of the secrets of past atmospheres and climate change. The ice traps tiny pockets of air, which scientists study. The trapped air contains a record of what the atmosphere and climate were like many years ago. German scientists are studying ice core samples of the world's oldest ice to show how the climate has changed. The ice core samples were taken from two miles (3.2 km) below the Antarctic ice sheet and are up to 750,000 years old.

METEORITES

Antarctica has many unusual meteorites. There have been more meteorites found in Antarctica than in the rest of the world. Most come from asteroid fragments, and some are "splash-offs" from Mars and the Moon as a result of asteroid collisions.

http://www.70south.com/resources/science/meteorites

http://library.thinkquest.org/26442/html/terra/meteorites.html

Compared with meteorites from other parts of the world, Antarctic meteorites are well preserved. The movement of the ice sheet gathers meteorites into special places, making them easier to collect.

This meteorite found in Antarctica came from Mars. Some scientists believe that some of its mineral features show signs of life on Mars.

FROZEN FACT
METEORITE HUNTERS
Scientists study aerial photographs of special blue-ice fields where meteorites are known to gather. They then search these areas using helicopters and Ski-Doos.

Using satellite images, scientists label huge icebergs that have broken off an ice sheet in the Antarctic so they can keep track of them.

GLOBAL WARMING

Antarctica is an ideal place to study global warming. Global warming is when the Earth's air temperature increases through human activity, such as burning **fossil fuels**. This releases greenhouse gases, which trap heat in the atmosphere.

Scientists measure the current temperature of the atmosphere over Antarctica and compare it to what they know about past atmospheres to look for changes. Scientists also study changes in the thickness, size, and speed of the ice sheet and glaciers to see the effects of global warming.

http://www.doc.ic.ac.uk/~kpt/terraquest/va/ecology/ecology.html

http://www.antarctica.ac.uk/About_Antarctica/FAQs/faq_02.html

THE OZONE "HOLE"

Every spring over the Antarctic, there is a thinning in the ozone layer of the atmosphere above the Earth. The ozone layer protects the Earth from harmful ultraviolet (UV) radiation from the Sun. The "hole" in the ozone layer contains up to 70 percent less ozone than normal.

Scientists discovered the ozone "hole" over the Antarctic in 1985. They have found that there is a cycle to the ozone "hole." After mid-November, the ozone comes together over the "hole," which reforms the following spring.

FROZEN FACT

iCE SATELLiTE
The National Aeronautic and Space Administration (NASA) Ice, Cloud and land Elevation Satellite (ICESat) takes regular three-dimensional images of the Earth's ice sheets to see how they are changing.

These long-extinct fossil leaves are found in all the continents that were once part of Gondwana.

http://website.lineone.net/~dave_reay/

http://www.science.org.au/nova/018/018key.htm

FOSSILS

Scientists have found fossils of long extinct dinosaurs and plants from a warmer and wetter time. Scientists study the fossils found on Antarctica and compare them with similar fossils from Australia, India, Africa, and South America. This helps to show that millions of years ago, Antarctica was joined with these places as part of a super-continent called Gondwana.

SOUTHERN OCEAN

The Southern Ocean surrounding Antarctica plays a major role in controlling the Earth's climate. Cold, dense water and nutrients from Antarctica travel along the seabed to warmer regions of the Earth. This helps to keep the world's ocean ecosystems working.

Scientists study many things in the Southern Ocean, such as pack ice, icebergs, wildlife, and seabed sediment and creatures. There is still a lot to explore and many unknown species. It is important that scientists provide accurate data on the Southern Ocean. This information is used to help manage the krill and fishing industries operating in the area.

FROZEN FACT

ANTARCTIC BOTTOM WATER
Cold, dense water called Antarctic Bottom Water is produced when winter sea ice forms in the Antarctic. This heavy water sinks to the seabed and flows slowly north, away from Antarctica.

Antarctic issues

Human activities, including exploration, have had impacts on the unique Antarctic environment and created issues for the **ecological sustainability** of the region. Today, there is global awareness that positive action is required to protect this wilderness area.

The Antarctic Treaty is used to manage Antarctic issues. It is a unique international agreement signed by 45 nations. The Antarctic Treaty and its conventions and **protocols** address Antarctic issues and protect the ecological sustainability of the region.

ANTARCTIC ISSUES AND SOLUTIONS

Seal and whale hunting The Convention for the Conservation of Antarctic Seals protects seals and manages hunting seasons. The International Whaling Commission (IWC) has stopped all commercial whaling.

Overfishing The Convention for the Conservation of Antarctic Marine Living Resources controls the harvesting of marine resources. It sets legal catch limits and tries to control illegal fishing.

Scientific bases and research Environmental impact agreements ensure garbage is removed and pollution is cleaned up.

Tourism Protocols on tourism control tourist activities and ensure that they leave nothing behind.

Introduced species Introduced animals are no longer allowed in the Antarctic.

Mining The Madrid Protocol banned mining for 50 years from 1998. It will be reviewed in 2048.

Global warming The Kyoto Protocol aims to reduce greenhouse gas emissions. Several countries are investigating forms of renewable energy, such as wind power.

The ozone "hole" The 1987 Montreal Protocol banned ozone-damaging chemicals. Ozone-friendly products are now mostly used.

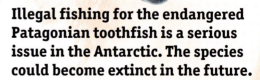

Illegal fishing for the endangered Patagonian toothfish is a serious issue in the Antarctic. The species could become extinct in the future.

SCIENTIFIC BASES AND RESEARCH

There are 74 permanent bases in the Antarctic. Pollution is caused by untreated sewage from bases, paints scraping off ships and falling into the sea, shipping accidents, and chemical spills. Garbage from bases can harm local plants and wildlife.

Scientific research may also disturb plants and wildlife, especially in sensitive areas. It can also increase the possibility of disease spreading to animal colonies.

Under the Antarctic Treaty, all garbage and waste has to be cleaned up and returned to the country of origin. The country operating a scientific base must also protect the surrounding environment.

Ship-based tourists are modern day explorers in the Antarctic wilderness.

TOURISM

In the past, tourists trampled plants, left waste, disturbed wildlife, and took souvenirs from heritage buildings and fossil sites. Tourist activity disturbed local ecosystems and threatened the pristine nature of the continent.

Today, Antarctic tourism is well managed. Food, water, toilets, and smoking are not allowed at landing sites. Tourist ships take all their waste with them. However, increasing tourist numbers place greater stress on the sensitive environment.

The future of the Antarctic

Antarctica holds the secrets to the Earth's past and could help us predict its future. Antarctic issues need to be fully understood and carefully managed. Many people would like to see Antarctica listed as a **World Heritage Area** where it would continue to be a model of peace and cooperation for the whole world.

http://www.antarctica.ac.uk/About_Antarctica/Conservation/

http://www.biosbcc.net/ocean/AAimportance.htm

http://bsauasc.nbs.ac.uk:8080/~nma/testsite//AboutAntarctica/Conservation/environment.html

Scientists from around the world work together in Antarctica.

ANTARCTIC COOPERATION

Antarctica is a unique place where scientists from all over the world live and work together in a spirit of cooperation in the wilderness. During the International Geophysical Year, from July 1957 until December 1958, scientists cooperated on many research projects. The success of this led to a permanent agreement on Antarctica, the Antarctic Treaty (1961). Scientists are exploring how the continent has changed over time and how it continues to change today and into the future. The results of their shared work may influence the future of the planet.

Glossary

circumnavigate	to sail around a body of land
crevasse	deep crack in a glacier formed as it moves over steep areas
cultural heritage	the remains from the past that are with us today. This can include human remains, tools, buildings, and monuments.
depots	places for the deposit of goods
ecological sustainability	the ability of the ecosystems to stay in balance now and into the future
extinction	when a species is no longer living
fossil fuels	coal, oil, and natural gas, which are derived from ancient life forms
geologist	a scientist who studies rocks
hydroponics	the growing of plants using chemicals mixed with water instead of soil
ice sheet	the thick layer of ice covering most of Antarctica; also called the Antarctic Plateau
ice shelves	layers of floating ice that are still attached to the mainland on three sides
pack ice	ice formed during winter when the surface of the sea freezes
protocols	first, written and signed agreements between nations
remote	a long way from other places
sextant	an instrument used for measuring the height of stars from a moving ship
sled	vehicle on runners, used to pull loads across snow and ice
soundings	when sailors took measurements of the depth of the sea with weighted ropes
species	types of animals
sub-Antarctic islands	islands surrounding Antarctica
valley glaciers	slow-moving rivers of ice
World Heritage Area	special areas with outstanding natural and cultural values that are important to the world and have to be protected for the future

Index

A
air transportation 22
Amundsen, Roald 12–13
Antarctic Treaty 18, 23, 28, 29, 30

B
Byrd, Admiral Richard 17, 22

C
climate change 25, 26, 28
clothing 21
communications 21
Cook, Captain James 5, 7, 8

D
d'Urville, Captain Dumont 8

E
Ellsworth, Lincoln 17
Enderby Brothers 7
exploration issues 29

F
first airplanes 16–17
first helicopter 22
first land crossing 19
first sightings and landings 6
food 21
fossils 10, 27
future 30

G
global warming 26, 28

I
International Geophysical Year (IGY) 18, 19
issues 28–29

L
Lake Vostok 24
land transportation 23

M
Mawson, Sir Douglas 11, 14–15, 16
meteorites 15, 17, 25

N
navigation 23

O
ocean transportation 22
ozone "hole" 26, 28

P
phantom islands 7

R
resource use issues 28
Ross, Captain James Clark 9, 10

S
satellites 17, 21, 23
scientific exploration 4, 5, 8–9, 10–11, 14, 15, 18–19, 24–27
Scott, Robert Falcon 10, 11, 12–13, 14, 16
sealers 5, 6–7, 28
Shackleton, Lieutenant Ernest 12, 14, 15, 16
shelter 20
Southern Ocean 4, 5, 7, 20, 27
South Pole 5, 11, 12–13, 14, 17, 19
sub-Antarctic islands 5, 6, 20, 21

T
transportation changes 22–23

W
Weddell, James 7, 8
whalers 5, 7, 10, 28
Wilkes, Lieutenant Charles 8
Wilkins, Sir George Hubert 16